words of
peace
for
Women

words of
peace
for
Women

Carolyn Larsen

R
Revell
a division of Baker Publishing Group
Grand Rapids, Michigan

© 2020 by Carolyn Larsen

Published by Revell
a division of Baker Publishing Group
PO Box 6287, Grand Rapids, MI 49516-6287
www.revellbooks.com

Printed in the United States of America

Library of Congress Cataloging-in-Publication Data
Names: Larsen, Carolyn, 1950– author.
Title: Words of peace for women / Carolyn Larsen.
Description: Grand Rapids : Revell, a division of Baker Publishing Group, 2020.
Identifiers: LCCN 2019028678 | ISBN 9780800736453 (paperback)
Subjects: LCSH: Christian women—Religious life—Meditations. | Peace—
    Religious aspects—Christianity—Meditations.
Classification: LCC BV4527 .L345 2020 | DDC 242/.643—dc23
LC record available at https://lccn.loc.gov/2019028678

20 21 22 23 24 25 26   7 6 5 4 3 2 1

1

The Source
of Peace Is Jesus

I have told you these things, so that in me you may have peace.
In this world you will have trouble. But take heart! I have
overcome the world.

JOHN 16:33

Peace is something everyone wants but most people find difficult to achieve. The reality is that life pulls away from and pushes against peace. Relationship trials, world situations, and even personal self-talk make peace a fleeting thing.

True, long-lasting peace comes from only one Source—Jesus. Think about what he says in this verse from John. He taught his followers about God and about his own work because if they could understand and believe his words, they could have peace.

You will have troubles in this world. That's a fact. Some will be big and overwhelming. Some will be daily annoyances. Both will disrupt your peace. However, keeping your heart focused on Jesus and knowing that he sees the big picture of your life and where things are going will alleviate your stress. There is no problem so big that he cannot handle it. No person is so powerful that he cannot overcome them. Jesus loves you more than you can comprehend. He knows what you're going through. He knows what's coming. He has it under control. Just trust him.

2

Representing Jesus

Blessed are the peacemakers,
for they will be called children of God.
MATTHEW 5:9

How do you see the line between taking a stand for the truths that define your beliefs and living in peace with others? The world is more defined than ever by different opinions. Biblical standards have become unpopular and divisive. Social media has provided a platform for ugly arguments to erupt. Is it important for you, as a believer in Jesus Christ, to be a peacemaker? If it is important, do you do that by keeping quiet or by joining the heated discussions, or are you somewhere in the middle? What's your guiding force?

Jesus says peacemakers are truly the children of God—what an honor to be called that! There is a way to stand up for biblical truths and be loving and kind at the same time. It's unlikely that a person will ever be argued into agreement, so why bother with that? Instead, speaking with respect, kindness, and love shows more of a likeness to Jesus and provides a pathway for a peaceful, intelligent discussion. Remember who you're representing and that Jesus called peacemakers the children of God. Ask for his help to stand firm while you represent him with love and kindness.

3

Strong Roots

*But blessed is the one who trusts in the L*ORD*,*
whose confidence is in him.
They will be like a tree planted by the water
that sends out its roots by the stream.
It does not fear when heat comes;
its leaves are always green.
It has no worries in a year of drought
and never fails to bear fruit.

JEREMIAH 17:7–8

Some situations in life not only steal your peace but also sap the energy out of your soul, or so it feels. For example, if you are in a bad relationship, whether it's a marriage, a friendship, a sibling relationship, or a parent-child relationship, the dailiness of dealing with those struggles is draining. Strength runs out. Hope of the relationship ever being better disappears. Peace is gone.

The lifeline available to you that will give you strength to get up each day in peace and hope and to keep on going is trust in the Lord. The image in these verses in Jeremiah is beautiful because the roots that began at the first signs of life of the tree have grown deep into the ground and now provide the nourishment the tree needs to survive.

When you accept Jesus as your Savior the roots of your faith in him begin to grow. Now, when you struggle, the strength of faith travels to your heart through those roots. This provides the nourishment you need to keep going each day in peaceful trust that God has things under control and that he will give you the strength and persistence you need exactly when you need it. Nothing can defeat you when your trust is in God.

4

Take the First Step

Joseph said to them, "Don't be afraid. Am I in the place of God? You intended to harm me, but God intended it for good to accomplish what is now being done, the saving of many lives. So then, don't be afraid. I will provide for you and your children." And he reassured them and spoke kindly to them.

GENESIS 50:19–21

If anyone had a solid reason to be angry, it was Joseph. His own brothers sold him into slavery then lied to their dad by saying Joseph had been killed by an animal. Joseph became a slave in Egypt, and then he became a prisoner when someone lied about him. But God used Joseph's position for good and he ended up a ruler, second only to Pharaoh, king of Egypt. Of course, even in that elevated position, he had lost his family—all eleven brothers and his beloved dad.

When his brothers came to Egypt to buy food so they wouldn't starve, Joseph could easily have tossed them in prison as payback for their awful behavior. But he didn't.

Throughout his life, Joseph tried to honor and obey God. At this point, he could actually see God's hand in all that had happened to him. He chose to forgive his brothers and live in peace.

Forgiveness doesn't come easily when you've been deeply hurt. Asking God to help you forgive and then allowing him to move in your heart is a choice. You must take the first step of asking God's help and then the first action of kindness, even if you don't "feel" the forgiveness yet. It will come.

5

Thief of Peace

Who of you by worrying can add a single hour to your life?
LUKE 12:25

What steals your peace? Does your peace disappear when you wake in the middle of the night and begin to worry about situations, people, or what-ifs? Worry may be the widest doorway into our hearts for the thief of peace. Why do we worry about things over which we have no control? Because we wish we had control? Sometimes we worry about how we'll handle a situation that may or may not happen. How much good does our worry do?

The answer to that question is none. Jesus said it: our worry does not add a single hour to our lives. It changes absolutely nothing for the better. Far better than worry is trust in God. When worry steals your peace, don't let it take root and consume your thoughts. Give it to God. Tell him what is causing your anxiety. Tell him all the what-ifs your mind is racing through. Ask him to remind you afresh of his love and care in your life. Allow yourself to see those reminders and to hold on to them when worry seeps back into your heart. He loves you so very much and shows that every day. Focus on that.

6

Peace in Submission

Father, if you are willing, take this cup from me; yet not my will, but yours be done.

LUKE 22:42

No one enjoys pain or suffering. Uncomfortable and troubling times can certainly usurp peace. What's your response when life gets difficult? Do you anxiously beg God to "fix" things so you can find peace again? Or can you find peace in the dark times through an attitude of trust and submission?

Jesus is your example for peace in times of struggle. As he prayed in the garden of Gethsemane, he asked God to take away the difficult times he knew were ahead of him. But, in trust and humility, he submitted to God's will. He believed that God's will was most important so he willingly faced all that was ahead, knowing it served God's greater purpose.

Lasting peace is only possible when your heart is submitted to God. Know that God's love for you is deep and constant and that his purposes are at the heart of all he does and allows. God's plan is not for you always to be comfortable but for his glory to be made known throughout the world. Find peace in being a part of God's great plan.

7

Heart Focus

You will keep in perfect peace
those whose minds are steadfast,
because they trust in you.

ISAIAH 26:3

What does the statement "What goes in is what comes out" mean to you? It could mean that if your diet is all junk food, your health and body will show the effects of a bad diet. It could also mean that if you fill your thoughts with what-ifs and worst-case scenarios, your heart will reflect those emotions and you will be consumed with fear and worry.

To keep fear and worry out of your heart, focus your thoughts on God. Start each day by reading Scripture and praying so you'll be reminded of God's power and strength. Focus on his great love for you and the many ways he shows you that love. Think about the ways he has cared for you in the past and remember that he knows everything you're struggling with, every decision you need to make, and each challenge before you.

When you keep your mind firmly focused on God, your trust in him will push aside fears and worries. A moment-by-moment awareness of God's power, strength, and love will keep your heart at peace.

8

Peaceful Nights

In peace I will lie down and sleep,
for you alone, LORD,
make me dwell in safety.

PSALM 4:8

Nighttime is the hardest, isn't it? The darkness, silence, and aloneness make worries and problems grow larger than life. When you're wide awake because of your worries the night seems interminable.

What can you do about the fears that assault your heart in the darkness of night? The right answer—though it isn't always easy—is to trust God. It's nearly impossible to keep your mind focused on God's loving care without his help. Ask him to help you by continually reminding you of his presence. Tell him what is worrying you. Verbalize your fears or write them down, and ask God to take the power out of the fears and to flood your heart with an assurance of his presence and protection.

Fill your heart and mind with Bible verses of God's love for you. Recall stories shared in Scripture of how he interacted with his people by protecting, guiding, and loving them. You know the truth of his care and love, but in the darkness of night, your heart may need to be reminded. Remember and then enjoy a night of peaceful sleep.

9

Teamwork

> *Do nothing out of selfish ambition or vain conceit. Rather, in humility value others above yourselves, not looking to your own interests but each of you to the interests of the others.*
>
> PHILIPPIANS 2:3–4

Life should not be viewed as a contest where you have the pressure of trying to outperform, outserve, outsucceed everyone around you. If you feel competitive about life, you will most certainly never have peace. When something good happens to a friend, you won't be able to celebrate with them because you'll be thinking about how you can top what just happened for them. How exhausting!

The reality is—and the Bible confirms—that life is not all about you, so be careful not to act as though it is. Everything and everyone does not revolve around you. God, in his grace, has placed you in a community not so you can compete with others but so you can become part of a web of support for one another. That happens when you celebrate others' blessings and empathize with others' sufferings.

The pressure you put on yourself to compete with others drains peace right out of you. God has unique purposes for each person, so jealously competing with others is futile. Humbly celebrate others' blessings instead of competing with them. You're part of a team striving for the same goal—the glory of God!

10

No Revenge

Do not repay anyone evil for evil. Be careful to do what is right in the eyes of everyone.

ROMANS 12:17

I t's human to want to get even. A human emotion—not a God emotion. Do you feel a sense of "justice is needed" if someone hurts or cheats you? Is it your responsibility to make sure justice is achieved? Is it your calling to bring someone before God to get what (you feel) they deserve? No, it isn't.

Scripture instructs you to do what is right in the eyes of everyone and, while you surely should not be a doormat to be treated badly by those who consistently behave poorly, you should also remember what Jesus taught. He said the second greatest commandment—of all the commandments in Scripture—is to "love your neighbor as yourself" (Matt. 22:39). Whew. That doesn't happen by getting even, judging, or criticizing. It happens by forgiving and moving on with your life while you let God handle that person's behavior. Jesus said to turn the other cheek (see Matt. 5:39), which means to be peaceable in a tough situation. There may also be times when you need to remove yourself from a situation or relationship. Do so with quietness and in a peaceful manner so that you don't fall into sin through your own behavior.

11

Don't Hold On to the Past

Forget the former things;
do not dwell on the past.
See, I am doing a new thing!
Now it springs up; do you not perceive it?
I am making a way in the wilderness
and streams in the wasteland.

ISAIAH 43:18–19

The only good thing that comes from dwelling on the past is learning from past mistakes and putting into practice what you've learned in order to make your present experiences better. Don't resent past failures; use them as lessons so that, with God's guidance, you'll grow wiser and more discerning.

If you focus on your past to the extent that it interrupts your present, you will not have peace in your relationship with Jesus. Focusing on your failures because you can't forgive yourself, even though Christ has already forgiven you, disrupts your ability to experience peace. Similarly, focusing on successes of the past instead of living in the present and seeking new victories also affects peace.

Be present in the moment. Notice the new things Christ is doing in and through you right this minute. Learn from the past but be present in the now, and celebrate all Jesus has taught you, is teaching you, and will teach you in the future!

12

Forgiving Others

Bear with each other and forgive one another if any of you has a grievance against someone. Forgive as the Lord forgave you.

COLOSSIANS 3:13

Holding a grudge against someone who has hurt you can seem like a good idea and a way to get back at them. But the reality is that it hurts you more than it hurts them. The energy it takes to hold a grudge or to hold on to anger saps your emotional energy and definitely steals your peace.

The better way to respond when you've been hurt is to forgive the offender then move on with your life. Of course that's not always easy to do. Ask the Lord to help you forgive and forget instead of seeking revenge. Begin praying for the person who offended you. It's hard to be angry with someone and pray for them at the same time.

Forgiving others is easier when you stop and think of how much and how often God forgives you. Remember his generosity in doing so and model that same behavior. When you let go of bad feelings, it makes room in your heart for more compassion, generosity, and love. It makes a healthier, more peaceful you!

Peace versus Envy

A heart at peace gives life to the body,
but envy rots the bones.

PROVERBS 14:30

A heart at peace is content with what it has. It's not easy to maintain contentment when the media and our culture are telling you that you need more or that you deserve more than what you have. That attitude makes you compare yourself to others, which then points out where you fall short. It builds envy into your daily thoughts.

Envy certainly steals peace from your heart because two such opposite emotions cannot simultaneously occupy the same space. Envy of others speaks of dissatisfaction with how God is treating you. What causes your envy? Do you feel God has not blessed you sufficiently? Has he not provided for your needs? Has he not gifted you enough or given you enough opportunities to serve him?

Envy keeps your heart focused on others, not on God. Turn your heart's eye to see his love for you and all the ways he shows that love. Focus on your blessings of salvation, family, friends, met needs, and opportunities he gives you to serve him. Recognize that all those opportunities are because of his unique plans for you.

Don't allow envy to rule your heart. Replace it with gratitude and humility, and peace will be the result.

The Thief Called Pre-worry

Do not worry about tomorrow, for tomorrow will worry about itself. Each day has enough trouble of its own.

MATTHEW 6:34

Are you an expert at pre-worry? Do you spend way too much time looking into the future and worrying about the possibilities of what could happen? Jesus says that pre-worry is a supreme waste of time. It takes you out of the present moment and robs you of the energy to enjoy the blessings God is showering on you at the moment.

This present day has worries enough of its own—things you must do and situations you must face. That means this day needs your full attention and energy. Instead of gazing into the future, be aware of the now—what God is doing in your heart and how he's leading you. Pay attention to the opportunities he is giving you this day. Be fully present in conversations and relationships of this day. Thank God for this day. Pray about the challenges of this day. Be assured that God will also be in tomorrow so there's no need to let your fears race ahead to it. Deal with *today* today, and deal with *tomorrow* tomorrow.

15

Your Heart's Treasure

Sell your possessions and give to the poor. Provide purses for yourselves that will not wear out, a treasure in heaven that will never fail, where no thief comes near and no moth destroys. For where your treasure is, there your heart will be also.

LUKE 12:33–34

You can say all the right words about what's important to you. Words that speak of your humility before God and your compassion toward those who are struggling in this world. Your words may be right, but your actions are what show the true feelings of your heart.

True concern for others will be evident in a few ways. One is by the way you spend your time. Is the greatest percentage of your life spent in efforts that are self-focused, accumulating more stuff, or building up your own reputation? Or do you spend time investing in others' lives through conversation or finding ways you can help them?

Another way your true self is revealed is through your finances. Rather than hoarding your money, giving it away to help those who have less shows real concern and compassion for them.

Blending your words with your actions eliminates the struggle between the two in your heart, which makes room for peace. If you don't feel compassion for others, then don't speak as though you do. Instead, speak to God, asking him to soften your heart and fill it with his love and care for others and to give you opportunities to put action to your words.

16

The Hiding Place

Every word of God is flawless;
he is a shield to those who take refuge in him.

PROVERBS 30:5

A soldier uses a shield to deflect arrows, spears—actually weapons of any kind—from hurting him. A shield gives protection in battle and sometimes saves a life. Of course a shield only helps if it is used. If the soldier leaves it lying on the ground, it's useless.

God has provided a shield for you. It's a place where you can safely hide to protect your heart from Satan's attacks and from the negative feedback the world may give you. That shield is him. He promises in his Word to always be with you, to hear your prayers, to give you strength and endurance. His Word is the handbook for living a life of faith in him.

God can be your shield only if you allow him to do so. Read his Word so you know what he promises. Submit your heart to him instead of struggling to control your own life.

Talk to him, asking for his guidance and protection. Huddle down in God. Trust him to protect you with his guidance and to give you discernment in decisions you must make. Celebrate his love and enjoy the peace you find in his hiding place.

17

The Gift of the Spirit

*I will put my Spirit in you and move you to follow my decrees
and be careful to keep my laws.*

EZEKIEL 36:27

How do you get to a place of peace in your heart? The source of peace is actually a loving gift from God—his own Holy Spirit. When you accept Christ as your Savior, the Spirit enters your heart and he is with you always. The Spirit's work is to convict you when you disobey God's commandments. He also reminds you of God's constant love for you. He moves your heart to submit to God and follow his plan for your life. Through all of those things and all of the other things the Spirit does, a possibility is provided for real peace in your heart.

The Spirit in your heart provides the strength you need to give your worries to God instead of obsessing about them yourself. The Holy Spirit's presence reminds you that God's power and strength are greater than anything you face. His love for you is powerful, constant, and deep.

Pay attention to the nudgings of the Spirit. He makes God's will known to you by clearly speaking to your heart and to your conscience and by giving you a peace about decisions you make and things you do.

18

Fretting over Evil

> *Do not fret because of those who are evil*
> *or be envious of those who do wrong;*
> *for like the grass they will soon wither,*
> *like green plants they will soon die away.*
>
> PSALM 37:1–2

Does it seem to you that the bad guys are winning? It's easy to get caught up in an attitude of desiring justice as you wonder why people who are unkind, dishonest, deceitful, or selfish seem to get ahead. Why doesn't God punish them or at least stop their bad behavior? Why doesn't God make sure the "good guys"—those who obey his commands—always win?

The basic answer to this question is that it's up to God to determine who succeeds. It's up to him to determine when people are punished or when their behavior is stopped. It's not your problem, though you certainly may be affected by their behavior. Just know that someday they will answer to God for their actions, just as you will answer to him for yours.

If you let yourself fret about evil people and whether they are punished for their behaviors, you'll have no peace in your heart. Trust God that justice will one day prevail. Trust him to care for his people in the way that he knows is best for them.

19

The Family of God

Let the peace of Christ rule in your hearts, since as members of one body you were called to peace. And be thankful.

COLOSSIANS 3:15

You belong to the family . . . God's family. When you accept Jesus as your Savior, you are adopted into the family. Think about the privileges of being in the family. You belong with the millions of others who follow Christ as Savior. That means you have millions of siblings! Now, if you have siblings in your earthly family, you know that life is not always peaceful with them. Siblings scuffle and compete and just generally bug each other.

It's not a good thing if that happens between the members of God's family. Your relationship with your Christian brothers and sisters should reflect God's love and peace. Your relationships should be an example to others of the bond of fellowship because of Jesus. They should be able to see patience, support, encouragement, love, and peace. It should be apparent that you have a singular purpose, and that purpose is to honor and glorify God and grow his kingdom.

Of course there will be differences; there always are in human relationships. But ask the Father's help in resolving them quickly and privately so that relationships are saved and God is honored by the love and peace of his children.

20

Slow Down

Be still, and know that I am God;
I will be exalted among the nations,
I will be exalted in the earth.

PSALM 46:10

One of the most common but biggest barriers to having peace is busyness. Have you ever tracked how much free time you have in your day or week? Time that is not dedicated to the next thing you have to do, but actual free time when you can let your mind rest and just be still?

If your life is crazy busy, make it a goal to carve out a few minutes each day to be still, and in those moments, think about God. Clear your mind of agendas and to-do lists and focus on his love for you. Think about how he cares for you. Notice the blessings, small and large, that he showers on you. Remember how he has guided you in the past. Recall times when you knew without a doubt that he protected you.

Thank him for the beauty of his creation, and tell him which parts bless you each day.

Slowing down your life and thinking about God's goodness and bigness will put your life in perspective. God is big. He is powerful. He is love. He will, and does, take care of you.

21

Your Heart's Throne

The LORD your God is a consuming fire, a jealous God.

DEUTERONOMY 4:24

The position of God in your life is often likened to a throne in your heart. The person or thing most important to you sits on that throne. If you're totally submitted to God, then he sits on the throne and your heart is generally at peace. If anything or anyone else is on your throne, peace is probably absent from your life.

You're either all in or you're out. God will not share your heart's throne with anyone or anything else. He is jealous for your love and your life because he loves you and knows that dedication to him is the true pathway to peace.

Remember playing musical chairs as a child? The game gets down to one chair with two players trying to sit on it. When the music stops, both players desperately try to sit on the chair, hip-bumping one another to push their opponent off. Trying to share your heart's throne between God and money, power, fame, people, or self is kind of like that. God will not play hip-bump with any of those other things. Stop trying to make that work. Give your heart totally to God and you will know peace.

22

Do Your Best

Whatever you do, work at it with all your heart, as working for the Lord, not for human masters.

Colossians 3:23

Why do you do what you do? Are you working for financial gain? To climb the corporate ladder? For popularity? Power? Appearances? What's your motivation? If your motivation is not coming from the right source, peace will not come with any success you think you've achieved.

The work you're doing, in whatever role it may be—dog walker, CEO, parent, teacher, waitress, student—any work at all, shouldn't be viewed as just a time filler until your "real" life begins. If you look at it that way, you'll grow impatient for the next step in your life—your "real" life. You'll miss opportunities to serve and glorify God. Whatever you're doing right now, wherever you are right now, is where God has placed you for this moment in time. Put your whole heart into the job you have today. Realize that whatever is before you today is what God has called you to do. Be at peace with that, and do it to the very best of your ability. Give it your all, and glorify God in the doing.

Rest for Your Soul

Come to me, all you who are weary and burdened, and I will give you rest. Take my yoke upon you and learn from me, for I am gentle and humble in heart, and you will find rest for your souls.

MATTHEW 11:28–29

What's weighing down your soul today? When you're worn down, it's hard to feel the sunlight on your skin, difficult to notice the birds singing or to enjoy much of life around you.

Rest, rejuvenation, and peace are available through Jesus. He loves you more than you can comprehend and is simply waiting for you to bring your weariness and chaos to him. Visualize laying your worries and problems at Jesus's feet, knowing that he can work them out and that he will lift the weight from your tired back.

There is no love gentler and more caring than the love of Jesus. No strength is more tenacious. No vision is deeper. He knows what's going on with you, and he cares when you're hurting and tired. He sees the whole of your life. He knows what lessons can be learned from your problems. His vision for your future is that you will have a deeper walk with him that is grounded in love and trust in him.

Are you tired? Look no further than Jesus for your rest. Give him your problems. Rest in his love. Be still and let him whisper into your heart.

24

God's Free Gift

When the kindness and love of God our Savior appeared, he saved us, not because of righteous things we had done, but because of his mercy.

TITUS 3:4–5

God's gift of salvation is a wonderful free gift to you. Did you hear that? Free! You don't have to work to earn it. You don't need to struggle to keep it. In fact, all you must do is ask Jesus to forgive your sins and then accept him as your Savior. He forgives your sin. He adopts you into his family. He gives you the Holy Spirit to live in your heart to guide you and help you throughout your life.

Don't get caught up in thinking you must do this or that in order to pay for your salvation. It's not a rental project where you must make monthly payments to keep it current. The total price was paid when Jesus died on the cross.

Jesus saved you because he loves you. He wants to have a relationship with you. He wants to take care of you, protect you, and bless you. This is all because of his mercy, which is another name for his care and compassion. Take the pressure off yourself, and relax in Jesus's love.

25

Leaving the Ninety-Nine

Suppose one of you has a hundred sheep and loses one of them. Doesn't he leave the ninety-nine in the open country and go after the lost sheep until he finds it? And when he finds it, he joyfully puts it on his shoulders and goes home. Then he calls his friends and neighbors together and says, "Rejoice with me; I have found my lost sheep."

LUKE 15:4–6

Does it seem foolish for a shepherd to leave the majority of his flock unattended (and therefore in danger) while he searches for one missing sheep? What if a wild animal attacks the ninety-nine? He could lose his whole flock or a big part of it.

It may seem foolish—unless you're the lost one. You may know the feeling of being alone, confused, lost. Your heart is in chaos because you're rushing one way then the next to find your way back to a place of peace and belonging.

This story shows the beauty of God's care not just for the masses but for the one . . . you. He cares so much for you personally that he searches for you when you're lost. When he finds you, he gathers you in his arms like a celestial hug and carries you back to safety. What's more, he celebrates that you are safely back with him. You're that important to him!

If you're struggling, you can be assured that God is reaching out to you, waiting for you to realize that he's there. Turn to him, don't run from him, and he will gather you up and carry you to safety. He cares that much for you.

26

God's Ways

> *"For my thoughts are not your thoughts,*
> *neither are your ways my ways,"*
> *declares the LORD.*
>
> ISAIAH 55:8

Why doesn't God do something?" Has your prayer time ever whittled down to that simple question? It's hard when you've prayed and prayed over something that you're struggling with but you don't see God taking any action. You keep hanging on because you have faith that God will answer your prayers. However, you realize that he may not answer in the way that you hope.

That realization takes you to the thought in this verse from Isaiah. God understands that your prayer is for him to solve the problem, to make things better, to heal the disease, to fix the relationship, to provide a job—whatever your situation is. But what you must understand is that he sees a bigger picture of life than you do. He sees how going through this problem can deepen your faith in him. He sees how this particular situation and your response to it can bring him glory.

Remember that your story is bigger than just what happens to you. Your story is part of God's story, and your role in it is to bring glory to him. What a privilege.

27

You're the Guest of Honor

You prepare a table before me
  in the presence of my enemies.
You anoint my head with oil;
  my cup overflows.

PSALM 23:5

When someone is unkind to you, what's your response? Do you want to get even? Do you want to bring down your "enemy" and make them suffer as much as they have hurt you? That's a very human response to an enemy. But thankfully, you can put your heart at rest because you don't have to worry about the whole "getting even" thing. God has it covered.

What could be more frustrating to your enemy than to have to stand by and watch while God throws a party in your honor? It's true, God serves up a fantastic feast with you as the guest of honor, and your enemy can't do one thing to stop it. That's what God does for you. As your enemies stand by silently, he celebrates you!

So let go of the urge to get even or demand justice when you have been hurt or slighted. It may take a while but justice will prevail. God knows what's happening. He knows who is being treated unjustly, and he will make things right. It may not happen today or tomorrow, but it will happen.

Keeping Good Company

"In the last times there will be scoffers who will follow their own ungodly desires." These are the people who divide you, who follow mere natural instincts and do not have the Spirit.

But you, dear friends, by building yourselves up in your most holy faith and praying in the Holy Spirit, keep yourselves in God's love as you wait for the mercy of our Lord Jesus Christ to bring you to eternal life.

JUDE 18–21

Are there doubts and chaos running rampant in your mind? Stop and think about the people you spend time with and the ones you listen to. Perhaps your unrest is a result of what is being fed into your mind. Think about it: if you've surrounded yourself with people who care more about their own wants and desires than about God's desires, their attitudes will seep into your life too. Even if you try to follow God, their attitudes will pull you away from him.

Keep yourself close to God to keep yourself close to God. Does that sound repetitive? It just means that in order to be close to God, you must conscientiously choose to stay close to him. Surround yourself with people who also desire to live for God. Read God's Word every day and look for how he speaks to you through it. Pray, telling God what's on your heart, what you're concerned about, where you need him. And thank him for all he does for you and gives to you. Make awareness of God's presence in your life a daily experience and see the chaos replaced with peace.

29

Obedient Trust

*"Do not lay a hand on the boy," he said. "Do not do anything
to him. Now I know that you fear God, because you have not
withheld from me your son, your only son."*

GENESIS 22:12

These are the words of God's angel to Abraham. God had
commanded Abraham to kill his son as a sacrifice to
God. Abraham and Sarah had waited a long, long time for
this child. His birth fulfilled a promise from God. Now God
wanted Abraham to sacrifice the boy? Did Abraham hesitate?
Did he argue with God? Not that Scripture tells us. His heart
was probably aching, but he obeyed God. So when he lifted
his knife to sacrifice Isaac, the angel stopped him. There was
no doubt that Abraham was completely, humbly obedient
to God. Abraham's peace, which was no doubt gone when
he faced killing Isaac, came flooding back when God said,
"Stop."

God may never ask you to do something as terrifying as this, but he does want your heart—all of it. If peace is elusive for you, could it be because you attempt to control your life instead of being completely submitted to God? Give him all your heart. Face whatever life brings. God sees it all. He wants to see your obedient trust in him, and he will take care of you . . . even in the hard times.

30

Seeking Peace

Whoever would love life
and see good days
must keep their tongue from evil
and their lips from deceitful speech.
They must turn from evil and do good;
they must seek peace and pursue it.
1 Peter 3:10–11

Do you want peace? Pay attention to how you treat other people. There will always be some folks who are not your favorites. There are those whose attitudes or negativity annoy you and those who know how to push your buttons to get a rise out of you. Don't let them.

A part of seeking peace may mean that instead of reacting to difficult relationships, you ask God to help you maneuver through them. Keep from speaking evil, which means refrain from voicing snarky comebacks or criticizing those who annoy you. Stop yourself from telling others of your frustration or even from padding the truth to make yourself look a little better (or a little more victimized).

Seek peace. Pursue it. Make it your goal. Don't strive to make yourself look good while pushing others down. Ask the Lord to help your focus stay locked on loving others as he has commanded you to do, even when it's hard. By doing that, your heart stays focused on him rather than on you, and peace will follow that focus.

31

Jesus Knows

For this reason he had to be made like them, fully human in every way, in order that he might become a merciful and faithful high priest in service to God, and that he might make atonement for the sins of the people. Because he himself suffered when he was tempted, he is able to help those who are being tempted.

HEBREWS 2:17–18

You cannot say, "No one understands. No one has gone through what I'm going through." It just isn't true. As difficult as it is to grasp, Jesus himself does understand. God, in his wisdom, knew that in order to convince people that he isn't just sitting up in his heaven apart from our reality, Jesus had to experience struggles that people face. He had to be fully human even though he is fully God. Yes, it's difficult to understand, but because Jesus experienced bullying, temptation, sorrow, and struggle, he understands when your heart is filled with chaos, and he can help.

Talk with him about your pain, struggles, fears—well, anything that is robbing your heart of peace. Ask him to guide you through the murky waters of struggle and to help you step onto the shore on the other side, safe and peaceful in his care. Jesus experienced these things so that he would understand. He doesn't want you to struggle alone. He cares. He can help. Ask him.

32

Never Give Up

> *Zacchaeus stood up and said to the Lord, "Look, Lord! Here and now I give half of my possessions to the poor, and if I have cheated anybody out of anything, I will pay back four times the amount."*
>
> LUKE 19:8

Have you been praying for a friend or loved one for a very long time? Are you asking not only for that person's salvation but also for their behavior to improve? Do you ask God to make them kinder, more responsible, or more honest? Maybe it feels hopeless after all this time and the angst in your heart has pushed peace aside. But don't ever give up. The story of Zacchaeus shows that no one is hopeless.

Zacchaeus was a hated tax collector who cheated people who were barely getting by. He took their hard-earned money for his own profit. Ugh. When the crowd of people who had gathered to see Jesus heard him say that he was going to

Zacchaeus's house, they were not happy. The guy was not nice. He had probably cheated all of them.

However, after talking with Jesus, Zacchaeus had a complete change of heart. He vowed to stop cheating, give half of everything he owned to the poor, and pay back those he had cheated—*four times* what he had cheated them out of! That's a big change.

Keep praying. Keep trusting. Don't let your heart get sucked into the chaos of feeling that Jesus doesn't hear. He does. He will answer in his own time.

33

Your Future Is Planned

The Lord himself will come down from heaven, with a loud command, with the voice of the archangel and with the trumpet call of God, and the dead in Christ will rise first. After that, we who are still alive and are left will be caught up together with them in the clouds to meet the Lord in the air. And so we will be with the Lord forever.

1 THESSALONIANS 4:16–17

Do you enjoy surprises or are you more comfortable when you know what the plan is? Does it make you anxious if you don't know what to expect?

Sometimes life is filled with surprises. That can't be helped. But there's one important plan you can rest assured will not be a surprise because it is God's promised plan. You can be confident that you will spend eternity with God in his heaven if you have accepted Jesus as your Savior. God's Word promises that truth. You need have no anxiety about your future. God's plan is revealed in the Bible.

If you are still living when Jesus returns, you will be reunited with your Christian loved ones who have died. Their spirits will go to heaven before you. Then you will join them in the air as you meet Jesus! What a glorious time this will be. Are there still unknowns? Sure. You don't know exactly when it will happen or what it will be like, but you can have peace in the assurance that it *will* happen. You will be with Jesus forever. He promises.

34

Jesus's Touch

A man with leprosy came and knelt before him and said, "Lord, if you are willing, you can make me clean."

Jesus reached out his hand and touched the man. "I am willing," he said. "Be clean!" Immediately he was cleansed of his leprosy.

MATTHEW 8:2–3

Is there a voice in your mind telling you that you've been too disobedient to God for him to pay any attention to you now? Have you lived only for yourself, done things that hurt others, or generally been such a bad person that you feel Jesus wouldn't want to get his hands dirty with you? Well, that feeling must keep peace in your heart at bay.

Here's the good news—nothing you've done shocks Jesus. Nothing in your past will make him turn away from you, step back from you, or completely walk away. Nothing. Why? Because he loves you that much.

In the story recounted in Matthew 8, Jesus did the unthinkable . . . he touched a leper. He put his hand on a man suffering with a highly contagious disease. Jesus could have spoken the words of healing. He didn't have to touch the man. But think of how long it had been since the leper had felt a human touch him. What surprise and joy Jesus's touch must have given him.

Whatever your past holds, call out to Jesus today for healing. He will touch your heart and heal it, and you will find peace.

35

Daily Choices

Turn from evil and do good;
seek peace and pursue it.
PSALM 34:14

You have a choice to make each day—each moment of each day, in fact. You can intentionally choose to do good and to seek peace in your heart, or you can slide through each day without committing to anything. Except, when you're sliding you *are* committing—just not necessarily to obeying God.

There will always be things around you trying to pull you away from God, good, and peace. The world will shout that you should make yourself number one, that life is all about getting what you deserve and everything you want. But that's not God's way.

To enjoy peace in your heart, choose to do good. That means choosing to obey and honor God. Listen to his guidance, seek his will. Obey him even when it's difficult. Love other people and consider them more important than yourself. Look for ways to serve others, to build them up, to encourage and support them.

The wonderful thing is that when you focus on serving God and others, your self-centeredness fades to the background because you have allowed honoring God and others to become more important than you are. The result is peace.

36

God's Whisper

> *A great and powerful wind tore the mountains apart and shattered the rocks before the LORD, but the LORD was not in the wind. After the wind there was an earthquake, but the LORD was not in the earthquake. After the earthquake came a fire, but the LORD was not in the fire. And after the fire came a gentle whisper. When Elijah heard it, he pulled his cloak over his face and went out and stood at the mouth of the cave.*
>
> *Then a voice said to him, "What are you doing here, Elijah?"*
>
> 1 KINGS 19:11–13

You have a crisis, a need for God to *do something*. You cry out to him over and over, begging for his intervention, stating your need, even telling him what you want him to do. Then you wait. No, you don't; you cry out again and again. Is God there? Is he paying attention?

Maybe you're looking for his response in the wrong way. Are you expecting to hear his voice in the strong wind? How about in the power of the earthquake? It's not there? Then maybe it's in the flames of the fire? No. God's voice comes as a gentle whisper to your soul because that way he knows he has your full attention. When he whispers, you must be quiet to hear him. You must shut out all other voices that are crying for your attention. Your focus is completely on him and on straining to hear his voice. It's a beautiful, personal time with God.

Keep crying out to him. Continue to ask him for answers, but make time to be quiet and listen for his voice. There is peace in his gentle whisper.

37

Forgive Yourself

I press on to take hold of that for which Christ Jesus took hold of me. Brothers and sisters, I do not consider myself yet to have taken hold of it. But one thing I do: Forgetting what is behind and straining toward what is ahead, I press on toward the goal to win the prize for which God has called me heavenward in Christ Jesus.

PHILIPPIANS 3:12–14

Your goal is to know God and grow better at serving and obeying him. But do you sometimes feel as though you take two steps forward and three steps back? Guess what—that's okay. You haven't arrived yet, so stop stressing. In other words, cut yourself some slack. Don't let failures steal your peace or discourage you from pursuing your purpose. Don't focus on failure. Stop looking backward at where you were a week ago or where you thought you'd be today.

You must keep moving forward. That means focusing on knowing God and serving him in submissive obedience.

Learn from your failures and mistakes. What do you do when you fail? Own it. Admit it. Confess it. Accept God's forgiveness. Forgive yourself, too, and move on.

You won't reach the goal God has called you to in a single day, month, or year. Learning to know God deeply is a journey, a process, and there will be good days and bad days. Don't give up. Don't beat yourself up. Learn and grow deeper in your faith and trust in God.

38

Stay Close to God

Submit yourselves, then, to God. Resist the devil, and he will flee from you. Come near to God and he will come near to you. Wash your hands, you sinners, and purify your hearts, you double-minded.

JAMES 4:7–8

You want peace in your life? Here's the pathway to it . . . stay close to God. This means more than showing up for church once in a while, reading your Bible every so often, praying when you want something. Staying close to God goes deeper than that. Submit to him, which means give him control of your life. Let go of your own plans and desires, and be willing to go do what God directs you to do.

Your heart and mind can't go in two directions at the same time, which means it really isn't possible to be fully submitted to God and not fight the devil. Satan will sneakily attract your attention and pull you away from your closeness to God.

So when you know he's pulling his tricks, intentionally and purposefully run away from him.

As you choose to submit to God and stay close to him, he will come close to you too. The reality of his love and guidance will be more apparent to you in everyday life.

God seldom pushes his way into your life. He allows you to choose him because then you are choosing to turn away from sin and flee from the devil. Choosing God is choosing peace.

39

Sharing Life

Two are better than one,
because they have a good return for their labor:
If either of them falls down,
one can help the other up.
But pity anyone who falls
and has no one to help them up.

ECCLESIASTES 4:9–10

Going through life alone is not easy. If you feel completely alone, finding peace in your life could even be difficult. Does this mean you have to have a family? No, but there is a benefit to having someone who walks through life beside you, even as a friend. It helps to have someone who will assist you, support you, and care about what you're going through. Someone who will laugh with you and cry with you. Even more important is having someone who will hold you accountable if you begin to wander away from obeying

God. Someone you will listen to when they challenge your decisions and choices.

Sharing experiences and challenges with a person God brings into your life is a blessing. Life is richer and deeper when it's shared. Sorrows are less deep when a friend grieves with you. Joys are greater when someone cheers with you.

When you struggle with faith issues, a friend will pray for you and remind you of ways God has shown himself to you in the past. A friend will help you stand again. Thank God for good friends and family, and celebrate the ways you share life together.

40

The Struggle for Peace

I do not understand what I do. For what I want to do I do not do, but what I hate I do. . . . As it is, it is no longer I myself who do it, but it is sin living in me. . . . Now if I do what I do not want to do, it is no longer I who do it, but it is sin living in me that does it.

ROMANS 7:15, 17, 20

If you've ever tried to lose weight, you may have a good visual of what these verses are saying . . . I want to eat healthy, but then I suddenly have a cookie in my mouth. Why do I let that happen?

If obeying God is the goal of your life, you may also relate to the struggle between desiring to obey God but so often doing just the opposite of what that means.

Sin actively pulls at your mind, heart, and behavior. Sin is part of who you naturally are and it, along with its originator, Satan, is always trying to pull you to the dark side, away from God.

This struggle steals your peace because it's difficult to be at peace when this war is going on in your heart. What's the answer? God is the only defense you have against sin. Ask him to help you recognize sin in your life. Then confess it, and ask him to help you turn away from that sin. You need his strength and awareness in your life to help you push sin out of your life.

41

Believe God's Love

Do not be anxious about anything, but in every situation, by prayer and petition, with thanksgiving, present your requests to God.

PHILIPPIANS 4:6

Don't be anxious? Right. For many people, anxiety is a part of life that's hard to escape. The world is chaotic. Careers are shaky. Health is elusive. Parenting is stressful. All these things and more present a multitude of opportunities for anxiety.

Resisting anxiety takes an intentional persistence to give your concerns over to God and trust him to take care of them. That's even deeper than simply praying about your concerns, because believing God loves you and depending on his power to work on your behalf are crucial to trusting his answers. So begin by examining your trust level. Do you honestly believe that God loves you? It's difficult to trust him if you don't believe in his love.

If you truly believe in God's love, then trust it. He tells you over and over again in Scripture how very much he loves you. So trust that he will answer your prayers in the way that he knows is best. Tell him your concerns and requests, and thank him as you're praying because you trust his response and his timing.

42

Mind Control

On my bed I remember you;
  I think of you through the watches of the night.
Because you are my help,
  I sing in the shadow of your wings.
I cling to you;
  your right hand upholds me.

PSALM 63:6–8

What you focus your thoughts on determines whether you have peace. When you lie down at the end of a busy day filled with work or family, struggles or joys, think about God. With the last thoughts of your day, thank God for his presence in your day. Recount in your mind his guidance, protection, opportunities—his very presence in your day. If your last thoughts before falling asleep are of God's loving care, you can sleep wrapped in the peace of his presence.

Take time each day to praise God for his care in your life. Praising him will help you remember how safe you are with the protection of his wings covering you. His powerful right hand holds you up, especially when you don't have the strength to stand on your own.

What you put in your mind plays a major role as to whether you have peace in your life. Focus on God's love, protection, and guidance. Fill your heart with him, and peace will be the result.

43

Living in Community

Peter was kept in prison, but the church was earnestly praying to God for him.

ACTS 12:5

Peter was in dire straits. He was in prison, guarded by sixteen soldiers. One of his friends had just been murdered, and it appeared that Peter might be headed for the same fate. Maybe Peter didn't know it, but his friends were together praying for Peter's safety, even in what seemed like a hopeless situation. God honored their prayers and sent an angel to miraculously escort Peter to safety.

When you are struggling in a hopeless situation or when you're buried in chaos with no peace in sight, you don't have to struggle through your problems alone. God has generously placed people in your life who will gladly pray for you. Don't discount the powerful prayers of God's people. Share your struggles with those close to you who will pray.

Be open and vulnerable enough to allow them to know when you need their prayers. Remember that God placed you in community for a reason. Share your life. Share their lives. Pray for one another, and live with God's peace in your heart.

44

Courageous Faith

Shadrach, Meshach and Abednego replied to him, "King Neb-uchadnezzar, we do not need to defend ourselves before you in this matter. If we are thrown into the blazing furnace, the God we serve is able to deliver us from it, and he will deliver us from Your Majesty's hand. But even if he does not, we want you to know, Your Majesty, that we will not serve your gods or worship the image of gold you have set up."

DANIEL 3:16–18

It doesn't seem like these three boys were even nervous about the possibility of being burned alive. Their hearts were fully devoted to God and therefore at peace with the decision to take a stand for him. Honoring God was more important to them than anything else, so they chose to honor him even if the consequence was death.

How strong is your faith in God? Would you stand firm even in the threat of punishment? Can you trust him even in the hard times? When he doesn't answer your prayers in the way that you ask him to, does your faith waver? When he seems to be silent, does your faith stay strong? When your faith is challenged by those in authority, do you hold firm? Is your heart at peace in all these situations because your faith and trust in God is completely firm?

Your peace will come when your faith is growing deeper and firmer. When your love for God and faith in him are more important to you than anything else, then whatever comes, your heart will be at peace in him.

45

Glorifying God

> He said to me, "My grace is sufficient for you, for my power is made perfect in weakness." Therefore I will boast all the more gladly about my weaknesses, so that Christ's power may rest on me.
>
> 2 Corinthians 12:9

Life often brings painful difficulties, and most people pray for God to fix the problem—heal the disease, provide a job, mend the relationship. Sometimes he does ... but what if he doesn't?

The apostle Paul had a problem or physical ailment that he asked God to take away several times, but God's answer was always no. Paul's response wasn't frustration or anger. No, he accepted that God's grace would help him cope with his problem. Whatever Paul suffered would bring glory to God because of the power he gave Paul to deal with it. Glorifying God was so important to Paul that he gladly accepted his plight.

Do you whine and complain about your difficulties, or are you willing to accept them? Have you considered that God's grace will give you the power to get through your problems and that he will be glorified through them? An attitude of submission allows you to seek God's glory over your own comfort. It's a recognition that the most important thing is not your comfort but for God to be honored and glorified.

46

Loving Others

Dear friends, since God so loved us, we also ought to love one another. No one has ever seen God; but if we love one another, God lives in us and his love is made complete in us.

1 JOHN 4:11–12

So much stuff gets in the way of us loving others. We make it a lot more complicated than it needs to be. We get caught up in what we feel is fair and what we want to happen. Egos get in the way, and we try to make people believe or behave the way we want them to. But is that really what it means to love someone? Or is that replacing love with control? God says to love . . . just love. Why is that so difficult?

Think about how much God loves you. He loves you just as you are. Of course, he knows that as you get to know him better, you will grow to become more like Jesus. But he doesn't insist that you already be like Jesus before he loves you.

Can you offer that same kind of patience to others? Can you love people just the way they are because loving them shows that God is living in your heart? If you need help loving some people, ask God to love them through you, and work with him on making that happen. Loving people instead of fighting with them will make your life more peaceful than it has ever been.

47

Peaceful Words

A gentle answer turns away wrath,
but a harsh word stirs up anger.
PROVERBS 15:1

You've probably heard the saying, "Count to ten before you speak." Do you practice it? It's a good place to begin if you want to live a peaceful life. Do you struggle to control your words? Do you tend to spout reactions or opinions without really thinking about how your words will make others feel? Are you critical of anyone who disagrees with you or thinks differently than you do about things?

Living peacefully with others is much easier if you consider how you speak with them. You should consider not just your words but also your tone of voice and how your words may be perceived. Ask a trusted friend whether you sometimes sound harsh and critical even when you don't mean to be. Try to not react quickly but instead think before you speak. Make it your goal to speak and react in love and kindness so that you can work with others and build relationships. Always remember that you are representing God in all you say. Ask him to help you think before you speak, and then speak with a gentleness and kindness that reflects his love.

48

Lessons from Discipline

No discipline seems pleasant at the time, but painful. Later on, however, it produces a harvest of righteousness and peace for those who have been trained by it.

HEBREWS 12:11

No one enjoys being disciplined. If you are disciplined, it means that you disobeyed a rule or instructions. It's embarrassing to be caught in this behavior. When you're disciplined, do you try to justify your actions? Do you defend yourself or maybe blame someone else? That kind of response doesn't go well when the discipline is coming from God, does it?

When you sense that God is disciplining you for something, think about why. What lesson does he want you to learn? What improvement or growth is he guiding you to experience? Of course being disciplined is tough, sometimes even painful. But if it wasn't, would you learn from it? God has more in mind than punishing you. He wants you to learn and grow when you are disciplined.

Instead of justifying your bad behavior or complaining about the discipline, look at what God may be trying to teach you. Ask him to help you learn. The result will be a deeper relationship with him as you grow more like Christ in your attitudes and behaviors. You will experience peace instead of frustration as you learn from the discipline God gives you.

49

Be Thankful

> "Come now, let us settle the matter,"
>   says the LORD.
> "Though your sins are like scarlet,
>   they shall be as white as snow;
> though they are red as crimson,
>   they shall be like wool."
>
> ISAIAH 1:18

Sin makes your heart dirty, and you can do nothing on your own to clean it. Sin keeps you apart from God. It prevents a close relationship with him because God is perfect and cannot have sin in his presence. But the situation is not hopeless. The dirtiness in your heart has been cleaned as white as snow by the generous grace of God.

Jesus took your sins on his shoulders and paid the price for them when he died on the cross. That completely cleaned the sin from your heart.

Don't discount this grace. Don't take Jesus's sacrifice for granted. You may feel that you're a pretty good person. After all, you've not murdered anyone or stolen large sums of money. But you are a sinner, and sin is sin. Don't get caught up in the temptation to justify your thoughts, words, or behaviors. Pastor Alistair Begg has stated, "[Our] sin must be absolutely horrendous if it takes the death of God's only Son to fix it."*

By God's grace and love, Jesus has paid the price for your sin. That gift has made your personal relationship with God possible so peace, grace, and love can fill your heart. Be thankful.

*Alistair Begg, "The Death of Jesus (Part 2 of 2)," March 23, 2016, Truth For Life, https://truthforlife.org/?date=3/23/2016.

50

The Battle for Your Heart

The Lord is faithful, and he will strengthen you and protect you from the evil one.

2 Thessalonians 3:3

Satan is real. He is constantly looking for ways to pull you away from God. He plants seeds of unrest and doubt in your heart. What chaos he creates in your mind!

But God is faithful. That means he's with you constantly—every moment of every twenty-four hours—whether you're asleep or awake, whether you're aware of his presence or not. He is with you. Think about that. You are never alone in the battle. Never. And God isn't just standing nearby, watching you struggle. No, he is involved. He is battling on your behalf. His strength is there for you to draw from. All you have to do is ask . . . and pay attention. Notice the ways in which you see his hand protecting and guiding you. Notice how Scripture verses or words of a favorite song remind you of his presence and his strength and power that will help you fight against Satan's attacks.

Let your heart rest in the truth that God is with you. Always with you. He is giving you the strength you need for each day. He is protecting you in ways that you may not even know about. He loves you so very, very much. Trust that love and rest in him.

51

Cherish Obedience

I cried out to him with my mouth;
his praise was on my tongue.
If I had cherished sin in my heart,
the Lord would not have listened.
PSALM 66:17–18

Do you wonder why you don't have peace in your heart? Maybe you need to examine the things that you cherish—the habits, thoughts, and actions that you hold on to. Are you cherishing sin by justifying your negative thoughts, words, and behaviors? Do you claim righteous indignation as your attitude toward anyone who holds different viewpoints from yours?

Remember that Jesus said the two greatest commandments—the two that encompass all the others—are to love God with all your heart, soul, and mind and to love your neighbor as yourself (Matt. 22:37–40).

If you can love God as completely as Jesus commanded, no room is left to justify bad behavior or anything that goes against Christlike behavior. If you love your neighbors as much as you love yourself, you will look out for them, encourage them, lift them up, cheer them on, give them the benefit of the doubt. After all, aren't these the things that you do for yourself? Doing these things leaves no room for anything but love.

Instead of justifying and cherishing sinful behaviors, confess them and repent of them. Make room in your heart for peace and joy as you love the way Jesus instructs.

52

Staying Strong

Blessed is the one who perseveres under trial because, having stood the test, that person will receive the crown of life that the Lord has promised to those who love him.

JAMES 1:12

You will have problems in life at some point. It's the nature of being alive and interacting with other people. How you respond to your troubles is important. Do you complain about your situation? Do you beg for relief? Do you just want your troubles to end?

The better response is to hold on tightly to God. He will walk through the problems with you and help keep your focus on his presence and on the good things that, by his grace, you are surrounded with. You can admit that things are hard or painful right now. But know that you will make it through your problems by being aware of God's presence and allowing his power to strengthen you. It always helps to know you are not alone. Staying focused on God will help keep your faith in him from wavering. Don't give up or feel that God has abandoned you.

Your peace during trials will come from knowing that God is not surprised by anything that's happening. By staying connected to him and trusting him, your heart will grow deeper in love with him. When you do walk closely with God, you will learn to persevere.

53

No More Fear

> *When you pass through the waters,*
> *I will be with you;*
> *and when you pass through the rivers,*
> *they will not sweep over you.*
> *When you walk through the fire,*
> *you will not be burned;*
> *the flames will not set you ablaze.*
>
> ISAIAH 43:2

Fear sucks the peace right out of your heart. When your heart is overwhelmed with fear, you feel so alone and hopeless. You look around for someone to rescue you, but everyone seems to be far away or not paying any attention to you. That just makes you more afraid. Fear also makes you self-focused because it's difficult to think about anything or anyone else. Survival is the primary goal.

Maybe you've experienced that kind of debilitating fear and aloneness. It certainly pushes peace from your heart. But this verse from Isaiah should bring comfort to your frightened heart. Look at the promises: "I will be with you," "the rivers . . . will not sweep over you," "you will not be burned," "the flames will not set you ablaze."

Absolutely nothing that happens to you is too big for God to handle. He does not step away from you, nor can he be pushed away. He will be with you. He is a boat for you in rough water. He is a shield protecting you from flames. God never leaves your side. You can trust him, and because of that trust your heart can be at peace.

54

Self-Talk

There is now no condemnation for those who are in Christ Jesus, because through Christ Jesus the law of the Spirit who gives life has set you free from the law of sin and death.

ROMANS 8:1–2

Your mind knows that when you accept Jesus as your Savior he forgives your sin—past, present, and future—as you confess and repent. That's wonderful, and it should settle your heart in peace; however, that peace doesn't happen if you keep beating yourself up over your past sins. Sometimes forgiving yourself is the hardest thing to do, but you won't have a peace-filled heart if you can't find a way to do it.

God doesn't condemn you for things you did before you knew him. He doesn't keep a record book of your new sins once you confess and repent. It's over and done with. In fact, Jesus paid the price for all of that sin. But what's that little voice in your mind saying to you? Do you condemn yourself over and over for things that God has forgiven? In order to know God's peace in your heart, you must let go of the past and forgive yourself. Ask God to help you forgive yourself for the past so that you can truly receive his forgiveness and know peace in your life.

55

Heart of Kindness

Get rid of all bitterness, rage and anger, brawling and slander, along with every form of malice. Be kind and compassionate to one another, forgiving each other, just as in Christ God forgave you.

EPHESIANS 4:31–32

A heart filled with peace is a result of living a life filled with God's love and forgiveness. Those around you can see the attractiveness of life with God by the peace, joy, kindness, and love in your life.

However, if you are harboring bitterness and anger in your heart, you will not have that God-attractiveness for others to see. The first step toward having peace is to learn why you have unhappiness in your heart. Can you figure out why you feel this way, then settle the issue so that you can allow positive emotions to take root in your heart? Maybe your issue is that you have an attitude of "me first" or a feeling of entitlement. Ask God to show you why you have unhappiness and bitterness in your heart and to help you let it go. Then allow him to help you begin to really care about people around you. Ask God to fill you with compassion for those who are hurting or lonely. Treat everyone with kindness, forgiveness, and a peaceful spirit, remembering that you are representing your God with each word you say and each thing you do.

56

Security

> *I am convinced that neither death nor life, neither angels nor demons, neither the present nor the future, nor any powers, neither height nor depth, nor anything else in all creation, will be able to separate us from the love of God that is in Christ Jesus our Lord.*
>
> ROMANS 8:38–39

It's difficult to have true peace in your life if you do not feel safe and secure. Peace comes with the confidence that you have placed your trust firmly in God and the relationship you've built with him is solid—nothing can rip it from your heart.

Of course, Satan continually attempts to disrupt your relationship with God and convince you that God doesn't actually care about you. His efforts definitely threaten the peace in your heart.

But as these verses tell you, there is nothing at all that can separate you from God's love. Nothing in this life or the next can pull you away from him. Once you belong to God, you always belong to him. He cares about you, and he never stops loving you. Trust him to hold you close. Trust him to help you fight off Satan's advances. Trust him to always have your back. Trust him to love you forever. Rest securely in your relationship with him. Don't let Satan steal your peace with his lies. He's wrong. He's always wrong.

57

Danger of Pride

Keep falsehood and lies far from me;
give me neither poverty nor riches,
but give me only my daily bread.
Otherwise, I may have too much and disown you
and say, "Who is the LORD?"
Or I may become poor and steal,
and so dishonor the name of my God.

PROVERBS 30:8–9

The peace in your heart can be stolen by you. If you become so full of yourself that you feel you do not need God in your life, your peace will be gone. Are you so self-sufficient that you push God over to the side and only call on him when you "need him"?

God's blessings should make you think about and trust him more. Unfortunately, the blessing of having plenty of what you need sometimes has just the opposite effect: you begin to feel that you're in control and you don't need God.

You even begin to feel that you deserve the blessings you receive.

Be careful not to dishonor God. Recognize that all the blessings you have—your salvation, the first breath of a new day, the food you enjoy, the friends and family you love, the job you have, even the privilege of knowing God and talking with him—are blessings he gives you. You do nothing to earn them. Keep your heart focused on God's gracious gifts to you and honor him. Peace will follow.

58

The Privilege of Prayer

As for me, I call to God,
and the LORD saves me.
Evening, morning and noon
I cry out in distress,
and he hears my voice.
PSALM 55:16–17

One of the greatest privileges you have as a Christian is that you can actually talk with your Creator. He wants you to do so. He even tells you to talk with him. Tell him what worries you, what frightens you, why you need his protection. He listens. He hears what you say to him and he cares.

The amazing thing, as the psalmist points out, is that God not only listens to your prayers, he answers them. He saves you from danger—probably more often than you know. He hears your cries of distress. Does this mean that you'll never have another problem if you cry out to God? No. He doesn't stop all your troubles. He doesn't do things in the way or the time you may want him to. But you will never go through tough times alone. He is with you each step of the way. He saves you by his power-filled presence, helping you put one foot in front of the other so you can keep going. And, in his perfect time, he answers every prayer in the way he knows is best. Talk with God about anything that's on your heart. Rest in the assurance that he is listening, he cares, and he will answer.

59

Singing Praise

About midnight Paul and Silas were praying and singing hymns to God, and the other prisoners were listening to them.

ACTS 16:25

Paul and Silas had problems. They were arrested for preaching about God. Then they were thrown into the middle of the jail where there was no chance for escape. They were chained up just to make certain they couldn't escape. It must have seemed like a pretty hopeless situation. But they didn't let their problems or their environment steal their peace. Instead of begging God to rescue them, they began singing songs of praise to him. No one could believe it. An earthquake happened, and Paul and Silas were set free— except they didn't leave the prison. They stayed so the jailer wouldn't be killed for letting them escape.

What an example these two men set of trusting God regardless of outward circumstances. They were a witness of God's peace to the other prisoners and to the jailer. Their trust in God led them to praise him and honor him in what seemed like a hopeless situation.

Can you trust God when life gets painful? Do you believe he will see you through the situation? Does your heart stay settled in peace because God promises to take care of you?

60

Memorizing God's Word

*I have hidden your word in my heart
that I might not sin against you.*
PSALM 119:11

God, in his gracious generosity and love, has provided what you need to get you through all of life. His Word gives you instructions for how to live in a way that pleases him. It explains how to treat other people. The Bible challenges you to serve God using the talents and gifts he has given you. God promises in his Word to always be with you, to protect you, and to guide you. He assures you that you're never alone because he is directing your steps each day.

The psalmist reminds you that memorizing God's Word—hiding it in your heart so it's always with you—will make its wisdom readily available to guide you in the decisions and choices you make in life.

With the promises of God's Word only a thought away, you'll be constantly aware of the Lord's presence in your life. The verses you recall will remind you of his power, strength, guidance, and deep love for you. So you need never fear or be lonely again. Realize the value of God's Word, and let its richness sink deep into your heart.

61

Life Experiences

I sought the Lord, and he answered me;
he delivered me from all my fears.

Psalm 34:4

When everything is going well in your life, you go about your days easily and you sleep peacefully. But when problems come, that peace is disturbed on all levels. It's hard to think about anything but your crises.

Where do you turn when you're frightened, troubled, or confused? Trying to fix things yourself seldom works. Friends can't solve your problems. Money, success, and power aren't the answers. There is only one way to find help and restore peace in your life . . . God. Call out to him. Tell him what you're struggling with. Ask him to guide you in the proper ways to restore relationships, improve your behavior, correct your attitude, or simply wait patiently for change.

God hears your prayers, and he cares about what you're dealing with. After all, he loves you. Remember that God sees a bigger picture of your life, and he knows when it's best to move you from one situation to another. God's desire is for you to learn and grow in your faith as you trust fully in him to get you through the experiences of life.

62

Stop Looking Back

I consider everything a loss because of the surpassing worth of knowing Christ Jesus my Lord, for whose sake I have lost all things. I consider them garbage, that I may gain Christ and be found in him, not having a righteousness of my own that comes from the law, but that which is through faith in Christ—the righteousness that comes from God on the basis of faith.

PHILIPPIANS 3:8–9

Living in relationship with Christ is a fluid learning experience. Things are constantly changing as he gives you opportunities to learn about him and to grow a deeper and stronger trust in him.

Sometimes in the faith journey you get caught up in grieving what you may leave behind. Whether you leave behind jobs, relationships, your health, or even your youth, some things are hard to let go of.

It may be hard to do, but it's important to keep your focus on Christ and the growth of your trust and faith in him. Don't let your peace be stolen because you're looking backward at what was left behind. Turn your eyes forward and see what you're learning through your present experiences. Trust Christ to put you in places where he can use you to do his work. Make it your goal to learn more about him, and let nothing be more important than that. Nothing you leave behind is better than what you gain by following and obeying Christ. Keep your heart focused on that goal and you will have peace, even in difficult times.

63

Your Secret Weapon

David said to the Philistine, "You come against me with sword and spear and javelin, but I come against you in the name of the LORD Almighty, the God of the armies of Israel, whom you have defied."

1 SAMUEL 17:45

What "giants" are you facing today? Are there things that seem too big for you to overcome? Some situations or people appear to be so powerful that their influence and oppression can't be battled. Young David could have felt that way when, armed with only a sling and stones, he faced the nine-foot-tall giant. He could have believed he didn't stand a chance against the giant, who had armor, a spear, and a shield. Except, David knew the full story. He knew that God was stronger than anything Goliath had. He knew that with just one swing of David's slingshot, God could take Goliath down. It was not going to be a long, drawn out battle where David would emerge victorious but bloody and exhausted.

God is stronger than anything you're facing today too. His love for you is deeper and stronger than any person's hatred for you. His plan for you is for good, not evil. Even if it seems that you're going into the battle with no armor and few weapons, remember that it is God who is fighting for you because you belong to him. So step courageously into the fight with peace in your heart and trust in God, who fights for you.

64

God and . . .

Do not worship any other god, for the LORD, whose name is Jealous, is a jealous God.

EXODUS 34:14

When you accept Christ as your Savior, you put him on the throne in your heart, so to speak. You give him your life, and your goal becomes to serve and obey him. But then life happens, and other things try to compete with God in their importance to you. If you don't pay close attention, you end up trying to make God and something else most important in your life. That never works. Your peace is destroyed because God is a jealous God, and he will not share your heart with anything else, even if that something else is a good thing in and of itself.

Examine your life. What fills your thoughts more than thoughts of God? What fills your calendar more than what God directs you to do? What absorbs most of your money? Answering those questions will show where your heart is focused. If the answers are not things God has told you to do, that could be the reason your peace is elusive.

Make the decision to recommit to God. Make him Number One in your life. Ask for his help to keep other things from taking over your heart. Your reward will be a heart filled with peace.

65

Real Peace

May the Lord of peace himself give you peace at all times and in every way. The Lord be with all of you.

2 THESSALONIANS 3:16

Where is peace in this war-torn, chaotic world? With nations divided against one another and people divided, friend against friend and family member against family member, where is the peace that the Bible speaks of so often?

There is no peace, nor will there be peace, apart from God. That means peace must begin with God's people. Peace begins in your heart. You can experience peace by submitting to God's direction in your life and trusting that he will care for you. If all God's people lived out his peace, wouldn't that difference in them be obvious to others? If others saw their willingness to be respectful to those with whom they disagree and their kindness, compassion, and humility, could this kind of behavior spread? Could it make a difference in the way people treat one another? Could it make the entire world a more peaceful place?

Your privilege as a God follower is to be an example of the power of God's peace and to show that his presence makes a difference in your life.

66

What Is Peace?

Cast all your anxiety on him because he cares for you.
1 PETER 5:7

How do you define peace? Many would say that the opposite of peace is chaos, often seen in your heart as anxiety or fear. A heart at peace would be calm, certain of safety and protection, because it trusts the One who rules it. A heart lacking peace is riddled with worry, fear, and anxiety—in other words, chaos.

To have peace in your life, you must first know God and trust that he loves you more than you can possibly imagine. He does. Scripture tells you that over and over. Then you must be willing to let go of control of your own life and humbly submit to whatever he wants. You can't trust if you don't believe his love. When you trust him, you know that he will help you through any bad things that come. He may not stop the problem, but you will never be alone as you walk through it. You can trust him because he loves you. That's the bottom line.

So, what does peace look like? It looks like trust in the One who loves you with a love that is deeper, fuller, grander than anything you can imagine.

67

The Good Shepherd

The one who enters by the gate is the shepherd of the sheep. The gatekeeper opens the gate for him, and the sheep listen to his voice. He calls his own sheep by name and leads them out.

JOHN 10:2–3

A shepherd takes care of his sheep. He protects them from the attacks of wild animals. He leads them to places where they can get food and water. He stays awake at night while they are sleeping just to make sure they are safe. The sheep follow the shepherd. They know the call of their own special shepherd, so they follow him and none other.

The Bible says that Jesus is the Good Shepherd and you are his sheep. He does all those things for you that a shepherd does for his flock of sheep. He protects you from the attacks of Satan. He feeds you through the wisdom and guidance of his Word. He nourishes your very soul with his care. He watches over you all the time. He never sleeps. So you don't ever need to be afraid; you only need to follow your Shepherd.

How do you learn to recognize the voice of your Shepherd? Spend time each day reading his Word. You'll learn what he teaches. Spend time praying and then being still to listen for his gentle whisper in your heart. The things you hear along with the things you learn from the Bible will help his voice stand out from all others.

68

True Relationship

Sacrifice and offering you did not desire—
  but my ears you have opened—
  burnt offerings and sin offerings you did not
    require.
Then I said, "Here I am, I have come—
  it is written about me in the scroll.
I desire to do your will, my God;
  your law is within my heart."

PSALM 40:6–8

There's a difference between religion and faith. Religion can become a confining set of rules that "someone" says you must keep. Any time you fail at that, you lose your peace and perhaps you feel you lose your relationship with God. Your faith-walk becomes a never-ending process of keeping rules and making offerings, and there can be times of guilt as you fail to keep some of the rules. A relationship with God is not a part of it.

But faith is based on a true relationship with God as your Father who loves and cares for you. As you grow to know him and trust him more fully, you want to serve him, to be a part of his work in this world. This doesn't happen because a rule says it must or because someone makes you serve God. It comes from your heart. You desire to do his will because you know he is the powerful Creator of the universe and his love for humankind is good.

Make sure that you have a relationship with God based on faith in his love for you. Don't settle for religion that offers nothing but rules.

69

Fighting Temptation

Jesus, full of the Holy Spirit, left the Jordan and was led by the Spirit into the wilderness, where for forty days he was tempted by the devil. He ate nothing during those days, and at the end of them he was hungry.

LUKE 4:1–2

If you've ever struggled with temptation, you know how wearing it is to stay strong against it. Temptation is like a constant drip of water, relentlessly steady until it wears you down and you give in.

Jesus understands the struggle of temptation. He was tempted by Satan for forty days, and during that time he didn't eat anything, so he was starving. That's a vulnerable condition to be in when you're tempted. Jesus didn't give in though. He quoted Scripture to fight off Satan's offers. And he resisted all the temptation.

Knowing that Jesus experienced temptation and was able to withstand it, even under dire circumstances, can give you strength to call on him for help. He's been there, so he knows what you're going through.

Scripture was important enough that Jesus quoted it, so that means it is important to commit Scripture to memory. Then, when temptation pulls at your heart, you can also quote God's Word to push it back and gain strength to not give in. Remember that you're not alone in the battle to stay strong. Have confidence in God's help and in the power of his Word hidden in your heart. He will bring it to mind just when you need it.

70

You're Not Perfect

Jesus said, "It is not the healthy who need a doctor, but the sick."

MATTHEW 9:12

News flash: You're not perfect. Does that shock you? You know when you sin. You know when you're self-centered, unkind, dishonest . . . any of a multitude of sins that work their way into your days. If you think only about your failures, you can get pretty discouraged. It can feel like you're not making progress in learning how to love God and others.

But don't get discouraged. Jesus knows that you're not perfect, and . . . great news . . . you don't have to be. He knows that the life of faith is a journey and that there will be good days and tough days. He even said that the reason he came to earth was to help the sick—those who need help in learning to follow God's commands. If you already did that perfectly, he wouldn't have had to come to earth and die for your sins.

God's grace has made a way for you to learn how to love and serve him. Jesus died for your sins. God has given you his Spirit to live in you and to teach you to obey him, to guide your choices, and even to pray for you when you can't find the words for your requests.

Jesus came for you because you need him and he loves you. What a wonderful plan.

71

Scary Requests

"Lord," Ananias answered, "I have heard many reports about this man and all the harm he has done to your holy people in Jerusalem. And he has come here with authority from the chief priests to arrest all who call on your name."

ACTS 9:13–14

Sometimes God asks you to do things that don't make sense to you. He may even ask you to do things that appear to be dangerous. If you aren't typically a risk taker, these opportunities may be a test of your faith. That will disrupt the peace in your heart.

Ananias knew about that. God asked him to help Saul, who later became Paul. But Ananias knew that Saul's life work was to persecute or imprison Christians. Why would God ask him to intentionally put himself in danger?

Of course, God had a plan. He knew that Saul had met Jesus and that his heart was changed, so Ananias would not be in any danger. Ananias had to trust and obey God, believing that God knew what he was doing.

Trusting God's heart, even in scary situations, is foundational to peace. He always has a plan, even if you can't see it. Whatever God asks you to do is for a purpose, and he will not make you go through it alone. Be thankful to be a part of his plan, and trust his heart.

72

Uniquely Gifted

If anyone thinks they are something when they are not, they deceive themselves. Each one should test their own actions. Then they can take pride in themselves alone, without comparing themselves to someone else, for each one should carry their own load.

GALATIANS 6:3–5

Do you get caught up in the comparison game? You know what that is—looking at people around you and ranking yourself compared to them. Are you doing better in one area, but they're doing better in another? It's exhausting and disturbing, and it keeps your heart in constant turmoil because you're always struggling to keep up with others or to push them down so you look better.

There's really no reason to play this game. God has gifted each person individually and uniquely to do his work in this world. All you have to do is obey him and work to the best of your ability. Remember that you are nothing apart from

Christ, so don't get puffed up with ego. You don't need to compare yourself to others. God isn't doing that. He's looking at how obedient your heart is. You will be much happier if you keep your eyes focused on God and do the work he gives you to do. Instead of pushing others down as you compare yourself with them, cheer them on. You and other believers are a team working together to do God's work.

73

Connected to the Vine

> *I am the vine; you are the branches. If you remain in me and I in you, you will bear much fruit; apart from me you can do nothing.*
>
> JOHN 15:5

What's your purpose? Since Jesus came into your life, has your goal become to honor and glorify him? If you're going to be successful in honoring and serving him, you cannot do it on your own.

Jesus is your lifeline. Through your relationship with him you get the spiritual nutrition you need to grow in faith. You receive his guidance for how to live your life. The reward for staying connected to him is that you bear fruit for him. That fruit shows an obvious faith in him, and that is a witness to those around you. It's evidence that you are a branch of his vine.

Trying to live for God in your own power will be pointless and frustrating and will not bring glory to him. You won't bear fruit for him. In fact, you will be attempting to bring glory to yourself, whether you realize that or not.

Stay connected to your Source. Read his Word each day. Spend time thinking about it and learning from it. Admit to yourself that apart from Jesus you are nothing and can do nothing for him. But, in him, you are everything. His power, strength, wisdom, and love are yours and will flow through you to others.

74

God Is Good

The LORD is good,
a refuge in times of trouble.
He cares for those who trust in him.
NAHUM 1:7

Bad things happen, even to good people. One of the scariest things that can happen is when the medical test results come back with bad news. Your life completely changes in just a moment as your time is spent with doctor visits, tests, treatments, and possibly hospitalization. The future is a big unknown, and that drains peace from your soul unless you can grab on to the truth of this verse.

God is good . . . all the time. Even when the test results are bad. He's good, even when things don't get better. He's good because he never leaves you alone to walk through scary things. He's good because as you take refuge in him, he teaches you about his care and compassion. He comforts you and strengthens you for whatever each day brings. He reminds you that your ultimate reward is with him in heaven for eternity.

Bad news puts your faith to the test. When it comes, you learn that you actually do trust God to get you through the experience. Each day is a new opportunity to see his love and care and to cry out for strength. God will never fail you.

75

Friend or Acquaintance?

You, God, are my God,
earnestly I seek you;
I thirst for you,
my whole being longs for you,
in a dry and parched land
where there is no water.

PSALM 63:1

o you seek God earnestly as the psalmist did? Does your whole being long for him? Is having a close relationship with him that important to you? Or are you content with being his acquaintance rather than his close friend? If you settle for being his acquaintance, you will miss many of the blessings of knowing him. One of those blessings is the refreshment his Spirit gives your hurting soul when you're struggling with problems. You'll miss the peace of knowing him well, recognizing his voice, and doing his work. You won't listen for his gentle whisper in your soul, telling you how much he loves you and how special you are to him. There is so much more relationship available to you than just being God's acquaintance.

Go deeper. Learn more. Understand more. Read his Word. Hide it in your heart. Trust more. Give him all your heart and life. Ask God to give you a thirst to know him and serve him. Let God be the answer to your questions, the guide for your life, the water that quenches your thirst. Let him be your all.

76

The Things of the World

Everything in the world—the lust of the flesh, the lust of the eyes, and the pride of life—comes not from the Father but from the world. The world and its desires pass away, but whoever does the will of God lives forever.

1 JOHN 2:16–17

You desire peace in your life? What do you value, the will of God or the things the world values? The things of the world are constantly thrown in your face as the things that are valuable or that signify success and pleasure. They are things that are all about you, not about God. Those things won't last forever—you can't take money or success or fame to heaven with you.

The only thing that goes to heaven with you is the truth of whether you chose to serve God with your life on earth. Did you seek to obey him? Were you careful that your attitudes, words, and behaviors honored him? Were you serious about sharing his love with others because you wanted them to know that he loves them?

You may put on a good show of serving God for others to see, but he sees your heart's motivation. Yes, if you have accepted Christ as your Savior, you do have the promise of heaven. But if you are living for your own glory and not his, he will see that also. Serve him out of love, not for show.

77

Active Faith

> *The woman, seeing that she could not go unnoticed, came trembling and fell at his feet. In the presence of all the people, she told why she had touched him and how she had been instantly healed.*
>
> LUKE 8:47

This woman had been sick for twelve years. She spent all her money on doctors to no avail. Because of her condition she was unclean, which probably kept people away from her and prohibited her from doing some of the things she wanted to do. Did she pray for healing? We don't know. We can surmise that her heart was filled with longing to be healed . . . to be normal. She took action and went to the one Person who she knew could help her. Regardless of how the people in the crowd that followed Jesus felt about her being around them or of the many people calling for his attention, she went to him. She believed—trusted—that healing could come from him. Her faith was so strong that she didn't even need him to speak to her. She believed that healing would flow to her by merely touching his robe. That's powerfully strong faith.

What has stolen your peace today? What are you longing for God's help with? You know where to go for the answers you need. Go to Jesus. Trust in his power to answer your need. Give action to your faith.

78

Doing Your Part

This is the confidence we have in approaching God: that if we ask anything according to his will, he hears us.

1 JOHN 5:14

The source of peace in your life is the Lord. Trusting his love for you is the foundation of your peace. Honestly believing that he will do what's best for your life is the proof of that trust. Do you share the apostle John's confidence that God actually hears your prayers? Do you trust that he will answer them? If you don't, why not? Can you look back in your life with him and recall times when he has shown his care for you? Can you see how God answered past prayers? Do you see how his answers were best—even when they weren't what you had prayed for?

Notice that there is one caveat in this verse, and that is that God hears your prayers when you are praying according to his will. How do you know what his will is? You must know him. Spend time reading his Word to learn his character and to learn what's important to him for the world and for you. Blindly shouting requests to someone you haven't gotten to know will not likely result in getting the response you desire. Do your part in building a relationship with God. Know him, talk with him, see his love for you in action, and trust will come . . . so will peace.

79

Think Positive Thoughts

Praise the LORD.

How good it is to sing praises to our God,
how pleasant and fitting to praise him!

PSALM 147:1

A wise person once said, "What goes in is what comes out." The thoughts you put in your mind are what will come out in attitude, words, and even behavior. If you're missing peace in your life, stop and think about what kinds of thoughts you're allowing to take up residence in your mind. Are you focused on negative, critical, or judgmental thoughts? Those will quite likely lead to similar attitudes.

How would things change if you focused your thoughts on praising God, beginning and ending each day by noting how God has blessed you, protected you, guided you, and loved you? Praise God every day for all he does for you. Praise him for the wonderful things *and* for the difficult things. Praise him for teaching you through the hard times. Praise him for his patience with you as you struggle to obey him and stay close to him.

Focusing your mind on praising God rather than on negative things will help you have more positive thoughts. It will also remind you daily of his presence in your life, which brings peace!

80

Stopping the Free Fall

The eternal God is your refuge,
and underneath are the everlasting arms.
DEUTERONOMY 33:27

o you ever have the dream in which you feel like your body is free-falling through space? You wake up with a start, your heart pounding, gasping for breath. It's not a pleasant way to wake up. Have you had a similar feeling about your actual life? There are times when it seems that God has allowed many of your supports to be knocked away through the death of a dear loved one, a lost job, a financial crisis, health issues . . . things that shake your security and make you feel that you're plummeting toward a dark, bottomless abyss.

That's scary, for sure. But it's also the time when you can actually realize God's love and support because in the middle of what feels like a free fall, his loving arms catch you. Go to God when you are scared, anxious, or frightened. Don't just turn to him, but run to him. Make him your refuge, the safe place where you can be protected from the attacks on your heart. Trust that his strong arms will safely hold you and stop the fall. Know that his love for you is deep and everlasting. You're safe with God.

81

Time-Out

The engulfing waters threatened me,
the deep surrounded me;
seaweed was wrapped around my head.
To the roots of the mountains I sank down;
the earth beneath barred me in forever.
But you, LORD my God,
brought my life up from the pit.

JONAH 2:5–6

Jonah . . . oh, Jonah. God told him to go to Nineveh and tell the people to stop sinning. Jonah didn't want the Ninevites to be saved, so he ran away. He ended up in God's time-out inside the belly of a big fish to think about his disobedience. That must have been an unsettling time. Three days in darkness, stench, and loneliness. He knew what he had done. Did he think he would be a goner if he didn't decide to obey God? Was he waiting for the fish's digestive juices to start kicking in? Well, God protected Jonah while he was in that time-out. He gave Jonah time to think . . . time to realize he needed to obey God. So, Jonah changed his mind, the fish spit him out, and he went to Nineveh.

There are times when you're waiting for God to do something, or perhaps you're stuck because you've not obeyed (or understood) some direction he has given. Those times of silence or static are good times for introspection and renewing your commitment to obey God. "Time-out" doesn't always mean punishment. Use it as a time to reflect, recommit, and learn.

82

No Yo-Yo Faith

Rejoice always, pray continually, give thanks in all circumstances; for this is God's will for you in Christ Jesus.
1 Thessalonians 5:16–18

At some time in your life, you may have played with a yo-yo—a small round toy with a string wrapped around the divided center of it. Rolling the yo-yo down the string and watching it roll back up is great fun. But, when referring to your faith-walk and trust in God, "yo-yo" is not a good description. Does your worship and praise come and go, depending on how easy your life is? Trusting him *sometimes*, praising him *sometimes*, and being thankful *sometimes* are not reflective of an honest, growing relationship.

God gives you wonderful things in your life and, no doubt, you praise him for those things. But when the hard times come, are you still able to praise him? Do you still rejoice? Do you continue to give thanks? Are your prayers more than

"God, do this"? If you give thanks for the good things, why not give thanks for the hard things too?

The faith to rejoice, pray, and be thankful always shows an understanding that God's will for you is good—not always easy, but good. Trusting his will gives you confidence and peace so that praise and thanksgiving flow . . . no matter what.

83

Spirit Guided

Since we live by the Spirit, let us keep in step with the Spirit. Let us not become conceited, provoking and envying each other.

GALATIANS 5:25–26

God's Holy Spirit lives in your heart. How that works is, indeed, a mystery. A blessed mystery. The Spirit speaks into your thoughts, guiding you to live by the commandments given in God's Word. He convicts your heart when your behaviors or attitudes do not reflect God's character. Paying attention to the Spirit's guidance and conviction helps you grow to be more like Jesus, and that is your goal. The Spirit helps you keep your focus on knowing and serving God so that you don't become self-focused.

It's difficult to be at peace with God and others if you're only thinking about yourself. Feeling that you're better than others or more important than others is not a way to show God's character to those around you. Think about how you're relating to others and whether you're helping them draw closer to Christ or causing them to fall away from him. Provoking or aggravating others is not what you should be about. You should be cheering them on, lifting them up, and encouraging them. Live in peace with God and others. Make it your goal to reflect God's love to others as you listen to the Spirit.

84

New Creation

> *If anyone is in Christ, the new creation has come: The old has gone, the new is here!*
>
> 2 CORINTHIANS 5:17

Suppose you have an old, beat-up car that has a multitude of mechanical problems. It's not reliable. It's ready for the junkyard. But you decide to give it a fresh coat of paint and try to pass it off as a good buy for someone. A coat of paint did not make it a new car.

Now think about your life. You were dead in your sin. You had no hope for heaven, no hope for a relationship with God, until Jesus died for your sins. When you accept Christ as your Savior, his sacrifice for your sins makes you a new creation. You don't just get a new surface, you get a new heart. You become new from the inside out. The old you is gone.

Are you living like the new person Christ made you? By seeking to know God more deeply, by honoring and obeying him, and by sharing his love with others, you show you are his new creation. If you're not doing those things, you probably have unrest in your heart because you know you're not honoring the sacrifice of Jesus.

Be true to your commitment to honor God. Keep the new creation in your heart shining through. Be the Christian Jesus allowed you to become by his death on the cross.

85

Believe Jesus

Do not let your hearts be troubled. You believe in God; believe also in me. My Father's house has many rooms; if that were not so, would I have told you that I am going there to prepare a place for you? And if I go and prepare a place for you, I will come back and take you to be with me that you also may be where I am.

If you've lived through the painful experience of losing a loved one to death, then Jesus's promise of eternal life takes on a new meaning. If you don't truly believe his promise, then the hope of ever seeing that dear one again is gone. Anguish and hopelessness fill your heart.

But look, Jesus said not to worry. He reminded his followers that believing in God means believing in him too. He had already told them that he was going to heaven to prepare a place for his family (Christians). Why would he have said that if it weren't true? He promised to come back and get his followers to come to heaven with him. He promised. If you believe God, you can believe Jesus.

The promise of being reunited with your loved ones who were believers is true. You will see them again. So, while your heart hurts that they are gone from this earth, you should not feel hopeless about the future. Jesus promised that he's getting your room in heaven ready. You will be together with your dear loved ones again.

86

The Plan

> "I know the plans I have for you," declares the LORD, "plans to prosper you and not to harm you, plans to give you hope and a future."
>
> JEREMIAH 29:11

Sometimes this verse is shared with the sugary sweet assurance that God has every step of your life planned. The idea of some is that the verse promises good, happy things, such as success and a long life. So if you're going through a particularly difficult patch in life, this verse can seem trite.

But think of it in a different way. After all, Jeremiah wrote this to a nation of people in exile. Their situation would not be considered prosperous or particularly hopeful. But there's always a reason for what happens in life. God does plan good things for you. But that doesn't mean that life will be easy by human standards.

God's plans are for you to grow deeper in your faith, for your trust in him to become more complete, and for your total dependence to be on him. Yes, God cares more about the depth of your soul than about what happens in daily life. Of course, he is always with you in the trials you face. He gives you strength and perseverance to get through them. Those experiences are what grow your faith.

So don't feel that God has deserted you in trials. He does have a plan for your life—to grow your faith in him, to make your heart kind and compassionate, to make you more like Jesus. Trust, learn, and grow. That's the plan.

87

Think Before You Speak

The tongue also is a fire, a world of evil among the parts of the body. It corrupts the whole body, sets the whole course of one's life on fire, and is itself set on fire by hell.

JAMES 3:6

Consider the fact that Jesus taught that you should love your neighbor. He taught the parable of the good Samaritan (Luke 10) to explain who your neighbor is: everyone, absolutely everyone. You can't live in peace with your neighbors without loving them and showing them kindness and respect. These characteristics are seen less and less often these days.

One of the ways a peaceful, loving relationship is apparent is in how you speak with others. Words are powerful. A harsh word can cut down a person. Critical, negative comments stick in a person's mind for a very long time—sometimes for a lifetime—holding that person back and keeping them pressed down instead of allowing them to grow and move forward. Relationships are destroyed by thoughtless words, gossip, judgments, and any words that damage another person's emotional or spiritual well-being.

Think about the words you speak to others. Think about the motivation behind the words you say. Are your words selfish, critical, or envious? Take time to think about how they will be received by the one who hears them. To keep peace in your relationships and with your God, think before you speak.

88

Helping One Another

Praise be to the God and Father of our Lord Jesus Christ, the Father of compassion and the God of all comfort, who comforts us in all our troubles, so that we can comfort those in any trouble with the comfort we ourselves receive from God.

2 Corinthians 1:3–4

When you are going through a difficult experience, do you ask God why? Do you wonder what could possibly be the good of having to endure such pain? Is your faith tested by those hard times?

Of course, when you cry out to God and ask him for the strength to make it through a crisis, he gives it, and eventually the whole experience is something in the rearview mirror of your life. But you learn new things about God's strength and care because of it. Then what?

These verses tell you that there may be a greater purpose for your pain than just your own experience. Often, after you've gone through something difficult, something that tested your faith, you meet someone else who is enduring a similar circumstance. Since you've been through something like what they are experiencing and you have known God's comfort and care, you can share with them how he helped you. So what you learned is passed along to someone else. You're part of God's family, and family members share with one another, encourage one another, and help one another.

89

Hope in the Lord

Those who hope in the LORD
will renew their strength.
They will soar on wings like eagles;
they will run and not grow weary,
they will walk and not be faint.

ISAIAH 40:31

Hope is important for experiencing peace in your life. If your hope is not solidly focused on the Lord, peace will be short-lived. On what is your hope focused? The world's culture and media tell you to hope in success, money, fame, popularity, getting ahead of everyone else . . . pretty much anything that makes life all about you. It's self-preservation and self-promotion. But none of that has eternal value.

Place your hope firmly in God. He will give you the strength to get through life, the perseverance to make it through dark times, the power to fight off temptation. He will give you compassion for those who are struggling. He will give you the energy to keep doing the work he gives you to do. It will be work with purpose, because you will have a part in furthering his kingdom on earth.

Your hope in the Lord will bless you with peace, even in hard times, because of his presence with you. There is nothing more important than hoping in God. Try anything else and you will not be satisfied. Something will always be missing.

90

Time to Move

Trust in the LORD with all your heart
and lean not on your own understanding;
in all your ways submit to him,
and he will make your paths straight.

PROVERBS 3:5–6

A loss of peace may not always be a bad thing. It might not be because of sin or disobedience that you begin to experience some dissatisfaction or unhappiness. Sometimes God moves you into a new ministry or a new way to serve him by allowing you to sense a certain amount of unrest in your current situation. Of course, he doesn't always need to do this. But if you have gotten quite comfortable with where you are and what you're doing, he may need to cause you to rethink what you're doing—in a job, in a ministry, in a location, or even in a relationship in order to get you to notice his guidance about moving to something new and better. Remember that things change in life as jobs are completed or situations change. Even as you grow older and more mature, God may want to use you in new places.

So, if you're experiencing a lack of peace, pay attention to other ways God may be trying to get your attention. Perhaps through Scripture verses that stand out to you, through the counsel of people you respect, or through your interests and thoughts. Follow his guidance and see what new and exciting things he has for you!

Carolyn Larsen is the bestselling author of more than fifty books for children and adults. She has been a speaker for women's events and classes around the world, bringing scriptural messages filled with humor and tenderness. For more information, visit carolynlarsen.com and follow her on Facebook.

Trust *God* and Live with Purpose

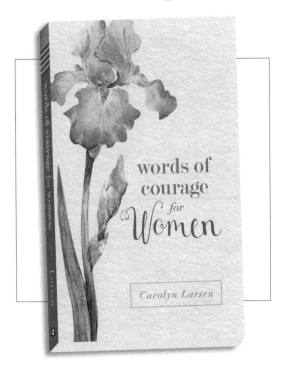

A 90-day devotional that will help you remember God's presence in your days and see your world from a positive perspective.

 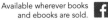

Reach Out to the One Who Promises *Comfort* amid Life's Trials

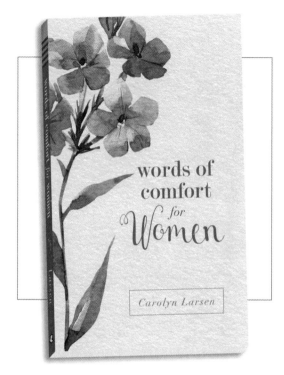

A 90-day devotional that encourages you during the challenges of life, offering comfort through the promises in God's Word and the people he places in your path.

 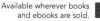

Find *Hope* through the Promises in God's Word

A 90-day devotional that will remind you that God has a plan and a purpose in everything—even the hard stuff—and you can trust him to keep his promises.